THE QUESTION BOOK

Also by Mikael Krogerus and Roman Tschäppeler

THE DECISION BOOK

THE QUESTION BOOK

WHAT MAKES YOU TICK?

Mikael Krogerus and Roman Tschäppeler

Translated by Jenny Peining

WITH ILLUSTRATIONS BY PHILIP EARNHART

W. W. Norton & Company

New York · London

The original edition was published in 2009 under the title *Das Fargebuch*
by Kein & Aber, Zürich
Copyright © 2009 by Kein & Aber, Zürich
Translation copyright © 2011 by Jenny Peining
First American Edition 2014

For information about permission to reproduce selections from this book,
write to Permissions, W. W. Norton & Company, Inc.,
500 Fifth Avenue, New York, NY 10110

For information about special discounts for bulk purchases, please contact
W. W. Norton Special Sales at specialsales@wwnorton.com or 800-233-4830

Manufacturing by Courier Westford
Production manager: Julia Druskin

ISBN: 978-0-393-24037-5

W. W. Norton & Company, Inc.
500 Fifth Avenue, New York, N.Y. 10110
www.wwnorton.com

W. W. Norton & Company Ltd.
Castle House, 75/76 Wells Street, London W1T 3QT

1 2 3 4 5 6 7 8 9 0

CONTENTS

INSTRUCTIONS FOR USE

This book started life with a really good question: Why do people so rarely ask a really good question?

This question turned into an experiment: What would happen if we compiled all the questions we'd ever wanted to ask, but for whatever reason had kept to ourselves? Questions that we kick ourselves afterwards for not asking, questions that get us thinking or make us laugh.

We discussed and debated, reflected and read. And above all we did something that we don't do often enough: we asked questions. The experiment turned into a book, which you are now holding: 616 provocative, stimulating, revealing, challenging, and eye-opening questions.

You can fill out *The Question Book* alone like a diary. You can use it to pass the time during a long train or plane journey—or use it as the basis for your memoirs! You can use *The Question Book* to find out whether you are reaching your potential at work, to lighten up a dull dinner party, or to draw a family member out of their shell. You can use it to spice up your relationship, or to finally get to know your parents—and it may lead to some heated discussions with your children. With this book you'll get even the shyest person talking. We believe everyone has a good story to tell: you just need to ask them the right questions.

Use *The Question Book* as you like: start from the back, scribble all over it, add your own questions. But don't expect any answers from us. The answers lie with you.

FOUR RULES OF THE GAME

1   Don't think about a question for too long; go with the first answer that comes into your head.

2   There are no right answers, only honest ones.

3   No answer is binding. It can always be revised.

4   We all admire people who have good answers. And we admire people who ask good questions even more. But most of all we are touched by those who can really listen.

THE QUESTION BOOK

LAST YEAR

Think about the last twelve months of your life and answer the following questions:

1 Your book of the year:

2 Your song of the year:

3 A film that you saw in the last twelve months:

4 Your item of clothing of the year:

5 The best sex:

6   The most important person:

7   The most annoying person:

8   A person you apologized to:

9   A person that you got to know:

10   A person you lost/left:

11   A person you neglected:

☐ A person who neglected you:

12 A bad argument:

13 Which of your friends did you see the most last year?

14 Who inspired you?

☐ Who did you inspire?

15 Something that changed your life:

16 The best gift:

17 An expensive purchase:

18 The best holiday:

19 A sense of achievement (at work):

20 The biggest disappointment:

21 Did you earn more or less or the same than in the previous twelve months?

☐ more ☐ less ☐ the same

22 A plan that you carried out:

23 How often were you ill in the last year?

24 The question of the year:

25 Something you learned:

Something you forgot:

26 A political event that moved you:

27 The party of the year:

28 Your quote of the year:

29 Your word of the year:

30 The wine of the year:

31   Something that surprised you:

32   The most difficult decision you had to make:

33   Something you regret doing:

34   Something you regret not doing:

35   Was this your best year so far?

☐ yes   ☐ no

☐ Why?

RIGHT NOW

36 Where are you right now?

....

....

37 Three things that you can reach without getting up:

a. ....

b. ....

c. ....

38 Two things that you did today:

a. ....

b. ....

39 Two people you've been thinking about a lot lately:

....

....

40   A word that . . .

■ describes your health:

....

■ describes your financial situation:

....

■ describes your work:

....

■ describes your sex life:

....

■ describes your relationship:

....

■ describes your life:

....

41   A magazine that you read regularly:

....

42 Your favorite pair of shoes:

....

43 Your perfume or aftershave:

....

44 Your favorite sport:

....

■ One that you like to watch:

....

45 Your favorite toy . . .

■ when you were a child: ....

■ today: ....

46 Which languages do you speak?

■ Fluently:

....

■ Well:

....

47 Which language would you like to learn?

....

48 On how many days of the week do you drink alcohol?

☐ none   ☐ 1–2   ☐ 3–5   ☐ daily

49 On what occasions do you avoid alcohol?

....

....

50 Three meals that you cook all the time:

a. ....

b. ....

c. ....

51 A meal that others enjoy eating and that you're good at cooking:

....

52 A meal that you would like to cook but have never tried to:

....

53 Approximately how much do you spend on food every month?

■ On groceries: ....

■ On eating out: ....

54 A TV program that you watch regularly:

....

55 The most famous person you've ever spoken to:

....

56 What is your nickname?

....

■ Who uses your nickname?

....

RITUALS AND ROUTINES

57   When do you normally go to bed?

☐ a.m.

☐ p.m.

58   When do you get up?

☐ a.m.

☐ p.m.

59   What is your favorite time of day?

☐ a.m.

☐ p.m.

■ Why?

....

60 Your sleeping position:

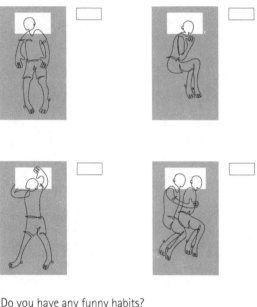

61 Do you have any funny habits?

....

....

62 What do you normally do when you are pondering a difficult decision?

....

....

63 What do you wear when you want to look attractive?

....

....

64 Describe a perfect evening.

....

....

....

65 A favorite ritual from your childhood:

....

66 Is there a ritual that you would like to start?

....

7 What ritual have you given up?

....

8 Other people's rituals that you find ridiculous:

....

....

▰ (GUILTY) PLEASURES

69   What do you usually order to drink at a bar?

....

70   When was the first time you got drunk?

....

....

71   Your favorite bar:

....

▪ Why do you go to this bar?

....

72   Your worst experience with drugs:

....

....

▪ Your most exciting experience with drugs:

....

....

73   What drug would you take if it didn't have any side effects?

....

74   Are you addicted to anything?

....

■ Can you deal with it or do you want to give it up?

[   ] can deal with it   [   ] want to give it up

75   Something that you used to be addicted to but aren't any
     more:

....

■ How did you manage to quit?

....

....

76   What do you do to treat yourself?

....

....

▨ COMMUNICATING

77   Mark on the diagram: How do you talk about . . .

- ▥ your day at work? (A)
- ▥ your holidays? (B)
- ▥ your achievements? (C)
- ▥ your partner? (D)
- ▥ your sex life? (E)
- ▥ your problems? (F)

78 Three words, phrases, or figures of speech that you use a lot:

a. ....

b. ....

c. ....

79 Can you express yourself better verbally or in writing?

☐ verbally   ☐ in writing

80 How many times a day do you check your email?

☐ once
☐ five times
☐ twenty times
☐ more than fifty times

81 How much time do you spend surfing the Internet every day?

....

▪ Do you think that's too much?

☐ yes   ☐ no

82   Are you on Facebook?

☐ yes   ☐ no

■ How many Facebook friends do you have?

....

■ How many of them would you describe as friends?

....

■ Do you post on Facebook? How often?

....

83   Who did you last write a letter to?

....

■ Who did you receive one from?

....

84   A speech or talk that you have given:

....

85   What do you have as your home page on your web browser?

■ www. ....

CAREER

36   What do you do for a living?

....

37   How would you explain to a child what you do for a living?

....

38   What do you define as work?

....

39   Why do you get up in the morning? Fundamentally speaking,
what do you really work for?

....

....

40   When you were younger, what did you want to be?

....

   ■ Why have you (not) become this?

....

91   What did your parents want you to be?

....

■ Why did you (not) become this?

....

92   What other career would suit you?

....

93   Besides your actual career, do you have other talents with
           which you could earn money?

....

....

94   What would be your ideal job if you didn't have to worry about
           money?

....

95   Do you have a career role model?

....

96 Mark on the line: What is more important to you?

career success <————————————————> personal happiness

■ What have you focused on more up till now?

....

■ Would you like to change this?

☐ yes   ☐ no

97 Describe a crucial turning point in your career:

....

98 Do you consider yourself successful?

....

99 "If you can dream it you can do it": According to your experience is this true or not? Explain.

....

....

100 Would you rather get a better salary or land a more interesting job?

....

101   Are your parents proud of what you do for a living?

      ☐ yes   ☐ no

    ■ Why? ....

    ■ Why not? ....

102   Would you recommend your children to pursue the same career path you have taken? Why?

....

103   In your relationship who is the breadwinner? What would change if your spouse were less successful than you?

....

104   If you have kids, how do you cope with the pressures of parenting on your work life?

....

....

105   Describe a situation in your career where you did not take the path of least resistance.

....

....

106   Take a look at your professional life: Did you envisage it like this?

....

107   Have you ever been unemployed? If yes:

▪ How did you become unemployed?

....

▪ How did you come to terms with it?

....

108   Are you a member of a union?

☐ yes   ☐ no

109   If yes, have you ever been on strike?

☐ yes   ☐ no

▪ If yes, why?

....

▪ If no, why not?

....

110   Do you also do voluntary work?

    ☐ yes   ☐ no

    ■ If yes, why?

....

....

    ■ If no, why not?

....

....

111   If you are retired, are you happy to be retired?

....

    ■ What do you miss?

....

....

112   Do you have a secure pension?

    ☐ yes   ☐ no

13 Mark on the diagram: all the jobs you have been paid for:

fun

well paid

badly paid

no fun

▆ IN THE OFFICE

114 What is the first thing you do when you get to your office?

....

115 What are the three things you are best at in your job?

a. ....

b. ....

c. ....

116 When are you at your most productive?

☐ morning ☐ afternoon ☐ evening

117 Do you work better under pressure?

....

118 Who would you ask to write a reference letter for you?

....

119 What aspects of your character are most in evidence when you're at work?

....

20   How many hours a week do you work on average?

....

☐ You would prefer to work less.

☐ You would prefer to work more.

21   Would you like to have more responsibility in your job or less?

☐ more   ☐ less   ☐ the same amount

22   Mark on the line: How demanding is your job?

too demanding ⟵—————————⟶ not demanding enough

23   Are you popular at work?

☐ yes   ☐ no

■ Why do you think this is?

....

24   What are your bosses doing wrong?

....

....

25   Would you rather work alone or in a team?

....

126   What position do you prefer on a team working on a project?

....

....

127   Who is your all-time favorite co-worker?

....

What do you like about him/her?

....

■ Who is your worst co-worker?

....

128   Name three friends you would like to work with.

....

....

....

129   What aspects of your job are you most confident about?

....

....

130 How far would you go in order to get a promotion/better job?

    a. Hide your religious beliefs..

    b. Tweak your résumé a little..

    c. Lie openly in a job interview..

    d. Go to bed with the employer..

    ■ Which of the above, if any, have you already done?

131 What gives you the greatest satisfaction at work?

132 What frustrates you the most?

    ■ How do you usually cope with it?

133 What do people most often criticize about you?

134 Have you ever experienced burnout or felt close to it?

135 What do you do in order to prevent burnout?

....

136 What have you done to improve your knowledge lately?

....

137 When did you stop thinking that you will become smarter?
Or do you still think you will?

....

138 Do you believe you will still be working for the same company
in five years?

....

139 How replaceable are you?

....

140 What inspires you about your job?

....

....

141 Who do you compare yourself to?

....

42 How much of your workday do you spend communicating via
email?

....

   ■ How much of your workday do you spend actually meeting
   with someone? Is there a difference?

....

....

43 What is your strategy for coping with too many emails?

....

44 Where do you typically sit in a meeting room? Do you have a
favorite spot?

....

45 Which company would you most like to work for?

....

   ■ What are the chances that one day you will work for it?

....

46 Which company would you never work for and why?

....

WHAT YOUR BOSS THINKS ABOUT YOU

Ask your boss!

If you can't or don't want to ask your boss, ask yourself: How would my boss answer?

Name of your boss:

....

147 Three things that I'm good at:

a. ....

b. ....

c. ....

148 How predictable am I?

unpredictable 0 _____ 5 _____ 10 predictable

149 How important is my role in the company?

unimportant 0 _____ 5 _____ 10 important

150 Do I earn too much, too little, or exactly the right amount?

■ Why?

151 How popular am I among my colleagues?

■ Why?

152 Something I should change about the way I work:

▨ BEING THE BOSS

153 Who is your favorite employee?

....

■ Why? ....

154 Who is your most important employee?

....

■ Why? ....

155 Look at your team: Who is missing (i.e., who would be good on your team)?

....

156 Which of these qualities in employees are most important to you? Rank them in order of importance.

a. Loyalty ....

b. Initiative ....

c. Reliability ....

d. Competence ....

e. Sympathy ....

f. Replaceability ....

157 What are you like? Rank the characteristics listed above in order.

....

158 Who was your favorite boss?

....

What did you like about her/him?

....

159 In your experience, what motivates employees?

....

160 What motivates you?

....

161 What is your greatest fear as a boss?

....

162 Who is your biggest competitor?

....

163 What do you admire in your competitors?

....

WHAT YOUR COLLEAGUE THINKS ABOUT YOU

Ask a co-worker. If you can't or don't want to ask one, then ask yourself: How would my co-worker answer?

164 Describe me in three words.

....

165 What does our boss think of me?

....

166 How popular am I among our colleagues? Explain.

....

....

167 What am I really good at?

....

....

168 What should I change about the way I work, or become better at?

....

....

MIND AND BODY

69 How many hours of sleep do you need?

....

■ How many hours of sleep do you get on average?

....

70 Your trick for getting to sleep:

....

....

71 How do you relax?

....

....

72 Would you like to be . . .

☐ slimmer?　　　☐ stronger?

☐ fitter?　　　☐ more dynamic?

173   How many times a day do you look at yourself in the mirror?

....

■ What do you see?

....

....

174   Do you exercise?

☐ yes   ☐ no

■ How many times a week?

....

■ Do you have the feeling you should be doing more exercise? If yes, why?

....

175   What was your most impressive sporting achievement?

....

176   Which sport would you like to be really good at?

....

179   Pinpoint . . .

- ▪ three problem zones.
- ▪ three physical features you are proud of.

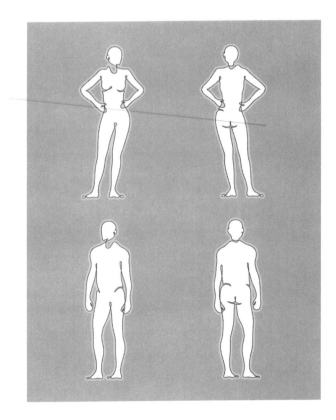

178 Pinpoint . . .

- three things that you like about your partner's body.
- three things that you don't like.

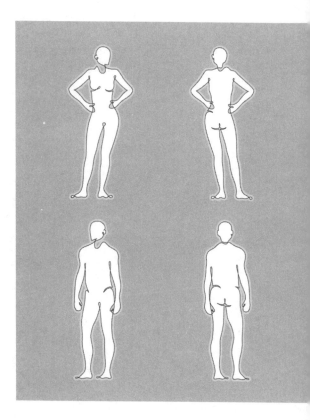

179 Have you ever been on a diet?

. . . .

  ▦ If yes, what kind?

. . . .

  ▦ How successful was it?

. . . .

180 How many times a week do you eat meat?

   ☐ never   ☐ 1–3 times
   ☐ 4–7 times   ☐ several times a day

181 Why are you a vegetarian/meat-eater?

. . . .

. . . .

  ▦ In your opinion, what distinguishes humans from animals?

. . . .

. . . .

182   What are your favorite cures or remedies?

....

183   What medication do you take regularly?

....

■ What medication do you think you should be taking?

....

■ Are you on a medication that you think you should stop
taking?

....

184   Do you have any phobias?

....

185   Mark on the line: How stressed do you feel at the moment?

relaxed ⟵—————————⟶ burnt-out

186   What helps you when you're feeling stressed?

....

....

187 Your worst illness:

....

....

188 Your worst accident:

....

....

189 The worst pain you've ever . . .

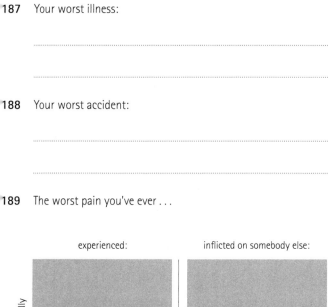

experienced: inflicted on somebody else:

mentally

physically

190   Can you imagine suffering from such an unendurable medical
          condition that you would consider committing suicide?

....

191   What age do you hope to live to?

....

192   What do you do to stay healthy?

....

....

193   Have you ever been in psychotherapy?

          [   ] yes   [   ] no

          ■ If yes, why?

....

....

194   Do you have medical insurance?

....

HOUSE AND HOME

195 How old were you when you moved away from home?

....

196 Do you prefer living alone or with somebody else?

☐ alone ☐ with somebody else

197 Think about all the people you have ever lived with.

■ Who was your best roommate?

....

■ Who was your worst roommate?

....

198 Draw the floor plan of the first home you owned.

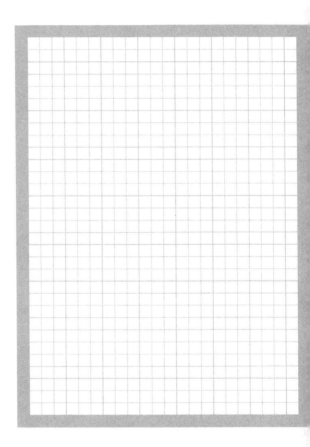

199 Which of your friends could you imagine sharing an apartment or a house with?

200 What percentage of your income do you spend on rent/ mortgage?

201 The nicest home you've ever lived in:

  ■ Address:

  ■ The nicest town you've lived in:

202 What is your favorite street in your town?

203 Where is your favorite place in your home?

204 Two things that you like about your home:

  a.

  b.

205 Two things that you dislike about your home:

a. ....

b. ....

206 Describe your dream home:

....

207 How would you like to live in old age?

....

208 Where do you feel at home?

....

209 Mark on the line below: What are you?

chaotic ⟵————————⟶ tidy

▨ Would you like to be different?

☐ yes   ☐ no

▨ Why have you not yet succeeded?

....

210 How many times a year do you get final demands for unpaid bills?

....

11 Household

	yes	no
▪ Do you always wash up right away?	☐	☐
▪ Do you vacuum every week?	☐	☐
▪ Do you have a cleaner?	☐	☐
▪ Do you do your own ironing?	☐	☐
▪ Do you clean your windows at least once a year?	☐	☐
▪ When the toilet paper is finished, do you immediately install a new roll?	☐	☐
▪ Do you tidy your home before visitors come?	☐	☐

▰ PICK YOUR THREE

212 Three places where you have lived:

   a.

   b.

   c.

213 Three of your favorite books:

   a.

   b.

   c.

214 Three films that you can watch again and again:

   a.

   b.

   c.

215 Three TV series where you haven't missed an episode:

   a.

   b.

   c.

16 Three music albums that have changed your life:

a.

b.

c.

17 Look at your iPod/iPhone: What were the last three songs that you played?

a.

b.

c.

■ What are the three most-played songs?

a.

b.

c.

8 Three games that you like to play:

a.

b.

c.

9 Three of your favorite drinks:

a.

b.

c.

220 Three brands that you like to buy:

a.

b.

c.

221 Three of your favorite local restaurants:

a.

b.

c.

222 Three things that are always on your to-do list:

a.

b.

c.

223 Three things that irritate you about other people:

a.

b.

c.

224 Three favorite topics of conversation at the moment:

a.

b.

c.

225 Three of your favorite shops:

a.

b.

c.

226 Three things you typically do when you're bored:

a.

b.

c.

227 Three things you would like to do before you die:

a.

b.

c.

CONFESSIONS

228 A film that really frightened you:

■ One that made you cry:

229 Something you know absolutely nothing about:

230 Something you spend too much money on:

231 Something that makes you happy:

232 Something that bores you:

33 Something you never want to do again:

34 Something that is sacred to you:

35 Music you like to listen to—but don't admit it:

36 One of the best concerts you've ever been to:

37 A work of art that inspires you:

38 An amazing experience you have had in nature:

MONEY AND POSSESSIONS

239 Your bank balance (approximately):

- Checking account: ....
- Savings account: ....
- Other accounts: ....
- Total _____

240 Your monthly income:

....

241 Could you survive on less money?

☐ yes ☐ no

242 Could you survive on half of your current income?

☐ yes ☐ no

243 How much do you earn compared to your best friend?

☐ more ☐ less ☐ about the same

44 Who do you owe money to?

....

45 Who owes you money?

....

46 What was the last thing you stole?

....

■ Why have you not stolen since then?

....

47 Have you ever been guilty of tax evasion?

☐ yes   ☐ no   ☐ don't know

48 Which three things (not people) would you save if your home was on fire?

a. ....

b. ....

c. ....

49 Something you have owned since you were a child:

....

250 Something you threw away/lost and would like to have back:

251 Something you should get rid of:

252 Something you would buy if you had the money:

253 Do you play the lottery?

    ☐ yes   ☐ never   ☐ only rarely

254 Do you own stocks or bonds?

255 Did you lose any money during the financial crisis? If yes, about how much?

    ■ Who do you blame? Yourself or someone else?

    ☐ myself   ☐ someone else

256 Have you ever been in financial trouble?

☐ yes ☐ no

■ If yes, why?

....

■ What did you do?

....

....

257 Who among your friends knows how much you earn?

....

258 Do you find it embarrassing to talk about what you earn? Why?

....

....

259 If you have a family, do you have a joint account?

☐ yes ☐ no

260 How much money will your children inherit when you die?

....

261 Fill in five valuable things that you own—according to monetary value and personal value.

+

monetary value

–

← personal value →

WHO YOU ARE

262   What nationality are you?

....

■ What common prejudices do people have against your
    nationality?

....

■ Which of these prejudices apply to you?

....

263   Two people who have influenced you:

....

....

264   Two events that have influenced you:

a. ....

b. ....

265 Your two best character traits:

a. ....

b. ....

266 Your two worst character traits:

a. ....

b. ....

267 Two compliments that you often get:

a. ....

b. ....

■ Which one means more to you?

◻ a. ◻ b.

268 Something hurtful that someone said to you:

....

....

69 What, for you, is a sign of independence?

....

   ■ Do you feel independent?

     ☐ yes   ☐ no

70 Do you think you act your age?

   ■ Yes, because

....

   ■ No, because

....

71 Something significant that has changed in your life in the last two years:

....

72 What are you currently struggling with?

....

73 What have you struggled with in the past but have learned to live with?

....

274 A behavioral pattern that you would like to change:

....

■ Why have you not succeeded?

....

....

275 An experience that you always tell people about:

....

....

276 Something you shouldn't tell people about but often do:

....

....

277 What do you spend too much time on, and what do you not spend enough time on?

■ Too much time:

....

■ Not enough time:

....

278   Two pointless things you spend time on but can't give up:

   a. ....

   b. ....

279   Two things you regret:

   a. ....

   b. ....

280   Two things you are proud of:

   a. ....

   b. ....

281   Which of the two previous questions was easier for you to answer?

   [＿＿＿] 279   [＿＿＿] 280

282   What moves you to tears?

   ....

   ....

283   Fill in the names of your closest relatives.

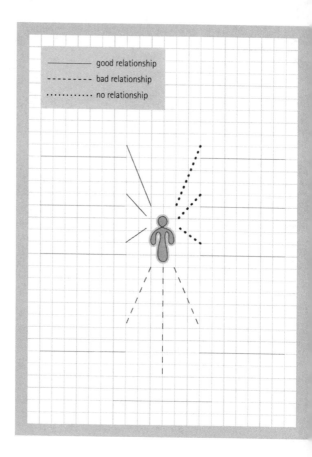

WHO YOU REALLY ARE

284 Would you describe yourself as a pessimistic or an optimistic person?

[   ] pessimistic   [   ] optimistic

- Why would you describe yourself in this way?

....

....

285 Describe a situation in which you felt out of your depth.

....

....

286 Describe a situation in which you felt insecure.

....

....

287 How loyal do you think you are?

disloyal 0————————5————————10 loyal

288 How reliable do you think you are?

unreliable 0 ——————— 5 ——————— 10 reliable

■ An occasion when you were unreliable:

....

289 How brave do you think you are?

cowardly 0 ——————— 5 ——————— 10 brave

■ An occasion when you were very brave:

....

■ An occasion when you were very cowardly:

....

290 Three skills you wish you had:

a. ....

b. ....

c. ....

291 Which of the following attributes could you use the most at the moment?

- [ ] persistence
- [ ] imagination
- [ ] courage
- [ ] calmness

292 What do you think you can do better than most of your friends?

....

293 When you receive a compliment, are you usually able to accept it and enjoy it, or do you feel you didn't deserve it?

....

■ Explain your answer.

....

....

294 In your relationships to date, have your partners loved you more than you loved them, or vice versa?

partner loves   ⟵————————⟶   you love
you more   partner more

295 In conversations with friends, are you usually the talker or the listener?

talker $\longleftrightarrow$ listener

296 What is your reputation among your peers?

....

....

■ Do you have a rival?

....

297 What effect do you think you have on others?

....

....

298 Would you like to have yourself as a friend?

☐ yes ☐ no

299 Are you a good loser?

☐ yes ☐ no

300 Can you cope with the feeling of being disliked by someone?

▨ Explain.

301 Have you ever hit your partner?

☐ yes ☐ no

▨ Your children?

☐ yes ☐ no

▨ In which situations?

MEN AND WOMEN

302 Indicate below: What is the first thing you notice in a man /
woman?

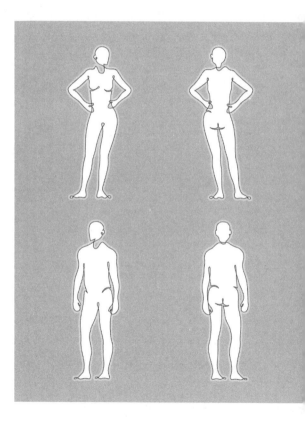

303 What are your most feminine qualities?

304 What are your most masculine qualities?

305 Do you have more female or male friends?

306 If you live with your partner, what household chores do you do?

307 Who do you think plays a more important role for the child?

308 Who has it easier in our society?

▪ Why?

309 Over the last thirty years, whose role has changed to a greater extent? The role of men or of women?

☐   ☐

■ Why?

....

....

310 How do you explain the fact that women in all Western countries still earn less than men?

....

....

311 Would you have your child operated on if your child was born with an unclear gender?

☐ yes   ☐ no

PRINCIPLES AND VALUES

312 Have you ever committed a petty offense?

▢ yes ▢ no

....

....

313 When, and how, did you last stand up for your beliefs?

....

....

....

314 What is the most overrated virtue? Give your reasons.

....

....

....

315 Have you ever read your partner's diary or emails?

....

■ Does your partner know about it?

☐ yes ☐ no

■ What did you discover?

....

....

■ Do you regret making the discovery?

....

316 When did you last tell a lie?

....

....

317 Do you lie to yourself? What about?

....

....

18 If you found out that the child you were expecting was going to be born with a disability, what would your reaction be?

....

....

■ What do you think your partner's reaction would be?

....

....

19 Do you have an organ donor card?

☐ yes ☐ no

■ If not, why not?

....

....

....

POLITICS AND BELIEFS

320 When you were younger, were you for or against the following . .

	for	against
▦ toughening up of the asylum system	☐	☐
▦ university tuition fees	☐	☐
▦ a divided Jerusalem	☐	☐
▦ war on terror	☐	☐
▦ state bailout of banks	☐	☐
▦ ban on adoption for same-sex couples	☐	☐
▦ legalizing doping in sports	☐	☐
▦ legalizing marijuana	☐	☐
▦ torturing of terrorists	☐	☐
▦ ban on smoking in restaurants	☐	☐
▦ nuclear energy	☐	☐

▦ What do you think today?

....

....

....

321 What is the biggest immigrant community in your town or area?

....

■ How many members of this community do you know?

....

■ Do you have any prejudices against this community?
If so, why?

....

....

22 What do you think are the three most important political
events to have occurred in your lifetime?

a. ....

b. ....

c. ....

23 Where were you when you heard about the 9/11 attacks?

....

■ What was your immediate reaction?

....

....

324 The three most pressing political issues:

a. ....

b. ....

c. ....

▪ What have you done for or against them?

....

....

▪ What would have to happen to spur you into action?

....

....

325 How would you attack the system if you wanted to destroy it?

....

....

....

26   Would you rather change the system or yourself?

☐ system   ☐ myself

27   Do you feel guilty about the conditions in developing countries?

☐ yes   ☐ no

28   Is there a political issue that you'd like to know more about?

....

29   Are you a member of a political party?

☐ yes   ☐ no

▪ If no, which party would you join if you had to?

....

30   What would you take to the streets for?

....

....

....

331   When did you last vote?

....

■   What did you last vote for?

....

332   Which politicians do you trust?

....

....

333   Are you patriotic, and if so, how do you express your patriotism?

....

....

....

THINKING GREEN

34 Do you sort your garbage?

☐ yes ☐ no

35 Do you use energy-saving electricity?

☐ yes ☐ no

36 Approximately what percentage of the food that you buy is organic?

....

■ Since when has this been the case?

....

37 What food-related health risks do you worry about the most?

☐ pesticides, toxic substances, viruses

☐ food additives

☐ lack of vitamins and minerals

☐ weight gain

☐ other (specify)

....

338 Are you concerned about how or where products are produced? Which products in particular?

....

....

339 If you drive a car:

■ Which make and why?

....

■ How much fuel does your car consume per 100 miles?

....

340 What would you be prepared to do to reduce your carbon footprint?

☐ get rid of your car

☐ change to energy-efficient electricity

☐ take the train when you go on vacation

☐ not eat meat for a year

☐ other (specify)

....

....

41   What do you think is the most pressing environmental issue?

....

■ What have you done about it?

....

....

■ If nothing, why not?

....

■ What would have to happen to spur you into action?

....

42   What luxury could you live without?

....

■ Why don't you?

....

....

FIRST TIME—LAST TIME

When was the first and last time you did the following?

First time

343	Fell in love
344	Dumped someone
345	Were dumped
346	Cheated on your partner
347	Were cheated on
348	Were drunk
349	Had sex
350	Had drunken sex
351	Were ashamed
352	Were the best at something
353	Lived alone
354	Took drugs
355	Thought about dying

Last time

◼ TRAVEL

356 Do you tend to pack too much or too little?

- [ ] too much
- [ ] too little
- [ ] too late

357 Three people you got to know while on vacation:
Are you still in touch with them?

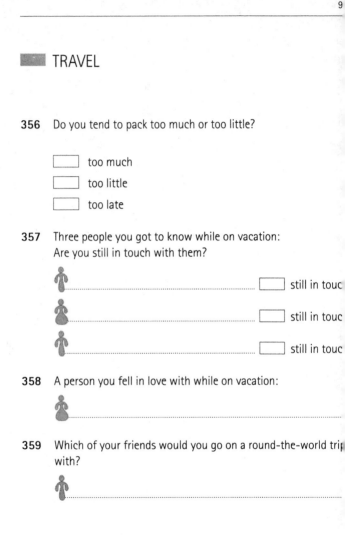

.... [ ] still in touc

.... [ ] still in touc

.... [ ] still in touc

358 A person you fell in love with while on vacation:

....

359 Which of your friends would you go on a round-the-world trip
with?

....

60 Your dream destination when you were a child:

....

■ Have you fulfilled this dream? How was it?

....

....

....

61 A vacation that went differently than planned:

....

....

....

....

362   Mark on the map:

- your best holiday (A)
- the last place you went (B)
- the next place you're going to (C)
- a destination that disappointed you (D)

■ where you would most like to go (E)

What would you like to see there?

■ ....

■ ....

363   Best of—worst of

   ■ The best hotel: ....

   ■ The best beach: ....

   ■ The best restaurant: ....

   ■ The most unfriendly country: ....

   ■ The nicest country: ....

   ■ The worst travel experience: ....

   ....

   ....

364   What do you miss when you're traveling?

   ....

365   The first thing you do when you get back from vacation:

   ....

CHILDHOOD MEMORIES

366 Your first memory:

367 A happy childhood memory:

368 A smell from your childhood:

369 A word that describes your time at school:

370 Who was your favorite teacher?

■ Why?

371 How would you describe your social class (as a child)?

- [ ] working class
- [ ] lower middle class
- [ ] middle class
- [ ] upper middle class
- [ ] upper class

372 How often did you move during your childhood?

....

373 Two friends from your childhood:

a. ....

b. ....

■ Do you know where they are today?

....

....

374 Two important books from your childhood:

a. ....

b. ....

375 The newspaper that your parents read:

376 A TV series that you grew up with:

377 Something you worried about when you were a child:

YOUR FAMILY

378 Who are you closer to: your mother or your father?

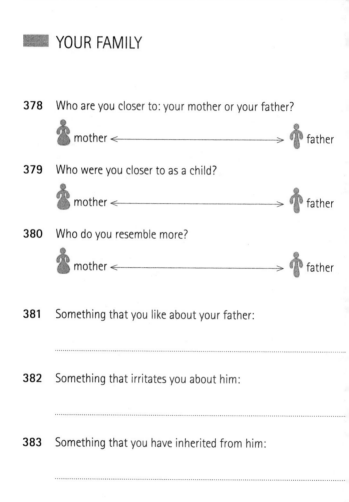

mother <————————————————> father

379 Who were you closer to as a child?

mother <————————————————> father

380 Who do you resemble more?

mother <————————————————> father

381 Something that you like about your father:

....

382 Something that irritates you about him:

....

383 Something that you have inherited from him:

....

384 Describe your father in three words.

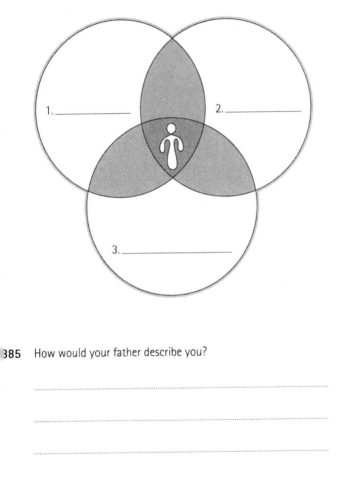

1. _____

2. _____

3. _____

385 How would your father describe you?

....

....

....

386 Something that you like about your mother:

....

387 Something that irritates you about your mother:

....

388 Something that you have inherited from her:

....

389 Describe your mother in three words.

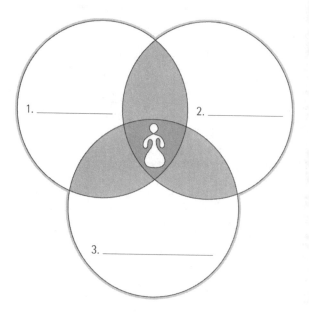

1. _____ 2. _____

3. _____

390 How would your mother describe you?

....

....

....

391 Who would you choose as your fantasy parents?

....

392 Were or are your parents happy in their relationship?

☐ yes   ☐ no

393 What do you admire about your parents?

....

....

....

394 What did your parents do wrong?

....

....

....

395 In what ways do you prefer your family to other families you know?

....

....

396 Are your parents still alive?

☐ yes   ☐ no   ☐ only one parent

■ If no, is there something you wish you had told them?

father: ....

....

mother: ....

....

■ If yes, how often do you visit your parents?

☐ several times a week

☐ two to five times a month

☐ two to five times a year

☐ other: ....

397 If you grew up in a "nontraditional" family . . .

■ what were the advantages?

....

....

■ what were the disadvantages compared to a "traditional" family?

....

....

398 Your favorite relative . . .

■ when you were younger:

....

■ today:

....

YOU AND YOUR SIBLINGS

Sibling A

399 In what ways are you alike?

400 In what ways are you different?

401 What do you like best about him/her?

402 What do you envy him/her for?

403 Favorite sibling:

404 If you weren't related, which sibling/s would you be friends with?

Sibling B

Sibling C

WHAT YOUR PARENTS THINK ABOUT YOU

Ask your mother or father.

If you can't or don't want to ask them, then ask yourself: How would my parents answer?

405 Was I a difficult child?

....

406 What did I love doing as a child?

....

....

407 How well suited to my partner am I?

not at all suited 0 _____ 5 _____ 10 very well suited

408 Do you worry about me, and if so, what do you worry about?

....

....

409 What do you think about what I do for a living?

....

....

410 Which of my achievements are you most proud of?

....

....

....

◼ LOVE

411 Do you love your partner?

[ ] yes   [ ] no

◼ How do you know?

....

....

412 Does your partner love you?

[ ] yes   [ ] no   [ ] don't know

◼ How do you know?

....

....

413 Do you feel desired by your partner?

[ ] yes   [ ] no

◼ Do you desire your partner?

[ ] yes   [ ] no

14   Three things that you value about your partner:

a. ....

b. ....

c. ....

15   Three things that you think your partner values about you:

a. ....

b. ....

c. ....

16   What would you describe as true love?

....

....

17   Try to predict: What do you think will be the biggest challenge
     in your relationship?

....

....

18   One of your partner's habits that you have to learn to accept:

....

419 Do you like your partner's friends?

☐ yes   ☐ no

■ 👤 These ones in particular:

....

■ 👤 These ones not at all:

....

420 What don't you like about your partner's family?

....

421 People tend to become more like their parents as they get older. Does this thought bother you in relation to your partner

☐ yes   ☐ no

422 In which situation do you find your partner odd?

....

423 Do you like yourself when you're around your partner?

....

24 Which of your weaknesses do you try to hide from your partner?

....

25 How much do you earn compared to your partner?

☐ more ☐ the same ☐ less

26 Something that you can't discuss with your partner:

....

....

27 Would you want your partner to confess to you if he/she had an affair?

☐ yes ☐ no

■ Do you confess your infidelities?

☐ yes ☐ no

■ Have you come to an agreement about being unfaithful?

☐ yes ☐ no

■ Does that mean you have affairs?

☐ yes ☐ no

428   If your partner were to cheat on you, would you prefer it to
be with a person you liked and found attractive, or a person
whose appeal you could not understand at all?

☐ attractive   ☐ unappealing

429   Is there a quality you wish your partner had?

430   Is there a quality you think your partner wishes you had?

431   What did you give up for the sake of your relationship, and
what do you miss the most?

432   Can you imagine continuing your relationship if your partner
became dependent on you or was radically changed through
accident or illness?

☐ yes   ☐ no

433   How is your current partner different from your last one?

34 How do you feel when your partner talks about their previous relationships?

....

35 Which of your ex-partners could you imagine getting back together with?

....

▪ Which one can you imagine sleeping with again?

....

36 Three ways in which you and your partner are alike:

a. ....

b. ....

c. ....

37 Three ways in which you are different:

a. ....

b. ....

c. ....

38 Which of the previous two questions was easier to answer?

☐ 436 ☐ 437

439   How often do you and your partner have sex?

....

440   Have friends more often advised you to split up or stay together?

☐ split up   ☐ stay together

441   In your relationships to date, have you usually done the dumping or been dumped?

☐ dumping   ☐ been dumped

▨ Why do you think this is?

....

442   If you are unmarried, would you like to marry?

☐ yes   ☐ no

▨ Why?

....

443   Which couples that you know do you find insufferable?

....

....

144 What do you think is the most common myth about love?

....

....

145 Are you romantic?

☐ yes   ☐ no

■ Back up your answer.

....

....

146 How do you think the Western ideal of romantic love is
connected to capitalism?

....

....

WHAT YOUR PARTNER THINKS ABOUT YOU

Ask your partner or an ex-partner.

If you don't want to or can't ask your partner, then ask yourself: How would your partner answer?

447 What was I like when we first met?

....

....

....

448 What am I like today?

....

....

....

449 Two things that you love about me:

a. ....

b. ....

50 Two things that irritate you about me:

a. ....

b. ....

51 In which situation(s) have you felt alienated from me?

....

....

....

52 Something that you have learned from me:

....

....

....

SINGLE LIFE

453 When and to whom did you last say, "I love you"?

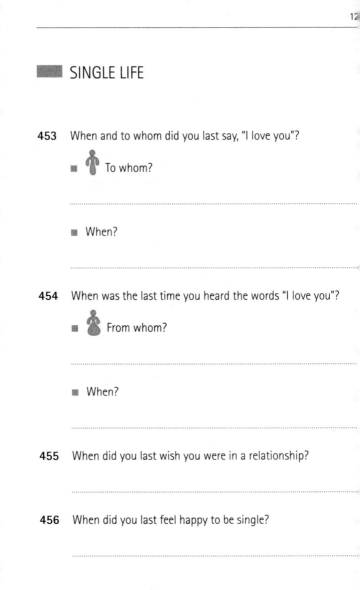 To whom?

....

■ When?

....

454 When was the last time you heard the words "I love you"?

■ From whom?

....

■ When?

....

455 When did you last wish you were in a relationship?

....

456 When did you last feel happy to be single?

....

457   Have you ever tried Internet dating or using a dating agency
(e.g., eHarmony, match.com, OkCupid)?

☐ yes   ☐ no

■ If yes, how was it?

....

....

458   Approximately how many of your friends are single?

....

459   For how much of your adult life have you been single?

....

■ Why do you think this is?

....

....

460   Your standard reason for explaining why you are not in a
steady relationship:

....

....

SEX

461 What type of man/woman normally falls for you?

....

■ What's your type?

....

462 A physical attribute that people often compliment you on:

....

463 What intellectual attributes do you find attractive?

....

....

464 How many sexual partners have you had in your life so far?

☐ 0–5	☐ 6–10	☐ 11–20
☐ 21–40	☐ 41–60	☐ more than 60

65 Somebody you regret sleeping with:

66 Somebody you regret not sleeping with:

67 An unfulfilled sexual fantasy:

68 A fulfilled fantasy:

69 Somebody you wanted but didn't get:

70 Somebody you wanted and got:

471   What are the advantages of monogamy?

....

....

....

■ What are the disadvantages?

....

....

....

472   Which of your close friends could you imagine sleeping with?

....

....

473   Which of your close friends could you imagine being in a relationship with?

....

....

474   What aspect of sex do you think is overrated?

....

....

475   How good was your sex life in the last three months?

bad 0 5 10 very good

476   What is the longest time you have gone without having sex?

....

477   How often do you masturbate?

....

YOUR FRIENDS

478 The friend you have known the longest:

479 Your newest friend:

480 Describe your best friend from when you were a child.

481 How does your best friend today differ from your best friend from childhood?

482 Your youngest friend:

483 Your oldest friend:

....

484 The last argument you had with a friend:

....

■ How did you resolve the argument?

....

....

485 Have you ever finished a friendship?

☐ yes   ☐ no

■ Why?

....

....

486 Did someone ever finish their friendship with you?

☐ yes   ☐ no

■ Why?

....

....

487 When was the last time you were a shoulder to cry on?

....

....

■ Who do you turn to when you need a shoulder to cry on?

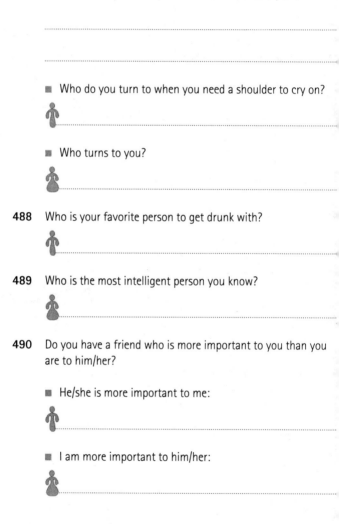

....

■ Who turns to you?

....

488 Who is your favorite person to get drunk with?

....

489 Who is the most intelligent person you know?

....

490 Do you have a friend who is more important to you than you are to him/her?

■ He/she is more important to me:

....

■ I am more important to him/her:

....

91 Which of your friends do you find attractive?

■ Which of your partner's friends do you find attractive?

92 Whose friendship could you do without?

■ Why do you remain friends?

93 Which friend that you have lost touch with do you still think about?

94 Which of your friends do you think know you best?

■ Who do you know best?

495 Have you ever hated someone?

☐ yes   ☐ no

■ If yes, why and for how long?

....

....

496 Who do you still need to apologize to?

....

497 Describe a situation in which you felt lonely.

....

....

....

498 Insert the names of five of your friends in the diagram.

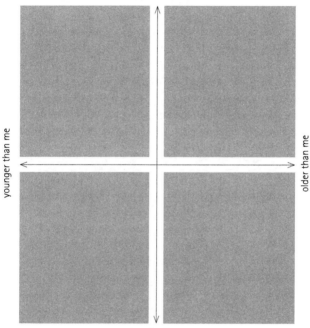

happier than me

younger than me

older than me

unhappier than me

WHAT YOUR FRIENDS THINK ABOUT YOU

Ask a friend who knows you well.

If you can't or don't want to ask your friend, ask yourself: How would my friend answer?

Name of friend:

....

499 What am I really good at?

....

....

500 What am I bad at?

....

....

501 What job would suit me?

....

502 What do I really need to learn?

....

503 Describe me in three words.

a. ....

b. ....

c. ....

504 Size me up.

- How brave am I?

cowardly 0 —————— 5 —————— 10 brave

- How reliable am I?

unreliable 0 —————— 5 —————— 10 reliable

- How happy am I?

unhappy 0 —————— 5 —————— 10 happy

MAKING DECISIONS

505 What do you listen to the most?

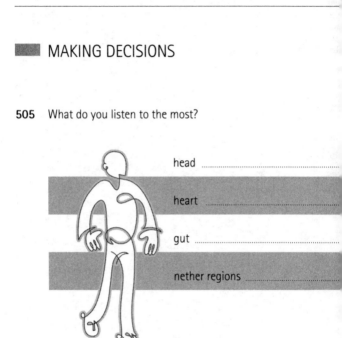

head ....

heart ....

gut ....

nether regions ....

506 A typical situation in which you are indecisive:

....

....

....

07 Who do you go to for advice?

....

■ A piece of advice this person has given you:

....

....

08 Who comes to you for advice?

....

09 Is there a decision that you've been putting off for a long time?

☐ yes ☐ no

■ Why are you unable to make the decision?

....

....

10 What was the best decision you made in the last five years?

....

■ What was the worst decision?

....

511   How often do you stick to your resolutions?

■ In your job:

☐ always   ☐ often   ☐ sometimes   ☐ never

■ In your relationship:

☐ always   ☐ often   ☐ sometimes   ☐ never

■ When it comes to your health:

☐ always   ☐ often   ☐ sometimes   ☐ never

512   Who makes decisions for you?

513   For whom do you make decisions?

THINKING ABOUT HAVING CHILDREN

514 Do you like children?

    ☐ yes   ☐ no

■ Do children like you?

    ☐ yes   ☐ no

■ Would you like to have children? How many?

....

15 What frightens you most about the idea of having your own children?

....

....

16 Would you rather have a boy or a girl? Why?

....

....

517   Have you ever seen your partner around children?

☐ yes   ☐ no

■ Did you like what you saw?

☐ yes   ☐ no

518   Do you know your partner's religious and spiritual convictions?

☐ yes   ☐ no

■ Are you in agreement about how your children should be raised when it comes to this issue?

☐ yes   ☐ no

519   Have you discussed who would be the children's primary caregiver?

☐ yes   ☐ no

520   Would you adopt children?

☐ yes   ☐ no

521   Would you consider having IVF?

☐ yes   ☐ no

522 What do you think about people who don't want any children?

....

....

523 What are the usual reasons you give for why you don't have children (yet)?

....

....

524 Which parents are role models for you?

....

525 If you could select your child's future career, what would it be?

....

....

BEING A PARENT

526 What are the advantages of having children?

....

....

What are the disadvantages?

....

....

527 Something you have never dared to do and that you hope your children would do:

....

528 Something you have done that you would advise your children against:

....

529 A piece of advice that you received as a child and that you followed:

....

530 How would you advise your children when it comes to . . .

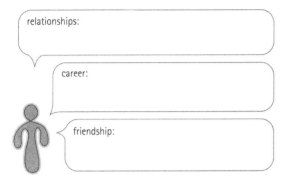

relationships:

career:

friendship:

531 What do you wish you had done differently with your children?

532 How have you changed since having children?

533 How has your partner changed?

534 How has your relationship with your partner changed?

....

....

535 What do your children think you do for a living?

....

536 Do you show favoritism toward any of your children?

☐ yes   ☐ no

■ Which one? ....

537 If you are a grandparent, do you think that your children are doing a good job of raising your grandchildren?

☐ yes   ☐ no

■ How does your children's parenting differ from yours?

....

....

....

HAPPINESS

538 What (if anything) is preventing you from being happy?

....

....

539 What is your advice to other people looking for happiness?

....

540 What are you looking forward to?

Today: ....

In general: ....

541 What obstacles have you overcome to find happiness?

....

....

542 What makes you unhappy?

....

....

543   Something that you usually do when you're . . .

unhappy: ....

happy: ....

544   A person you made happy:

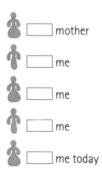

545   A person who made you happy:

546   A moment in which you were blissfully happy:

....

....

547   Who is happier?

A QUESTION OF FAITH

548 What do you believe in although you can't prove it?

....

....

549 A place where you go to recharge your batteries:

....

550 How spiritual are you?

not spiritual 0 _____ 5 _____ 10 very spiritual

551 What does it mean to you to be spiritual?

....

552 What do you think you were in your past life?

....

553 Something you dreamed about that came true:

....

....

554   Do you believe in . . .

- the apocalypse?   ☐ yes   ☐ no
- life after death?   ☐ yes   ☐ no
- fate?   ☐ yes   ☐ no
- the theory of evolution?   ☐ yes   ☐ no
- the self-regulating
  mechanism of the free market?   ☐ yes   ☐ no
- psychoanalysis?   ☐ yes   ☐ no
- astrology?   ☐ yes   ☐ no
- yourself?   ☐ yes   ☐ no

555   What is your star sign?

- What does it say about you?

- Do you agree with it?

☐ yes   ☐ no

☐ yes, apart from

556   What have you changed your mind about that you believed in
ten years ago?

557   What are your main doubts at the moment?

558 How did you find your faith?

559 How often do you pray and in which situations?

560 What is your religion and how do you explain your choice?

561 Describe a situation in which you questioned your faith.

562 What—in concrete terms—do you believe in?

563 Who believes in you?

564 What annoys you about the idea that there might actually be a God?

....

....

565 Have you ever been religious?

☐ yes   ☐ no

566 What prejudices do you have against religious people?

....

....

567 If you had to choose a religion, which one would it be?

....

568 What do you believe in if not in God?

....

....

569 Who believes in you?

....

FEARS AND ANXIETIES

570 What are you afraid of?

571 What are you no longer afraid of?

572 A frequently recurring nightmare:

573 What illness are you most afraid of?

574 Describe the most dangerous situation you have ever been in.

575 What has been the most difficult stage of your life so far?

■ How did you overcome it?

■ Are you afraid that you may experience something similar again?

☐ yes   ☐ no

576 Are you afraid of getting older? Why exactly?

....

■ Or are you looking forward to it? Why exactly?

....

577 What do you think old people are better at than young people?

....

....

578 Do you live the way you want to? If not, why not?

....

....

579 When was the last time you did something for the first time?

....

....

YOUR FUTURE

580 What will you be doing ten years from now?

■ Best-case scenario:

....

....

■ Worst-case scenario:

....

....

581 Who has an influence on your future?

....

....

583 Whose future do you have an influence on?

....

....

583 What goal are you currently most focused on?

....

....

■ When do you want to have achieved this goal by?

....

■ Will you reach it?   ☐ yes   ☐ no

584 What new skill would you like to learn?

....

585 Complete these sentences:

■ If I had more time, I would . . .

....

....

■ If I had less time, I would . . .

....

....

586   Do you have a life's ambition?

....

....

587   What do you most frequently dream of?

....

....

588   Have you ever had your fortune told?

☐ yes   ☐ no

■ Did anything come true?

☐ yes   ☐ no

■ If yes, what?

....

....

DYING

589 When was the last time you were at a funeral?

....

590 Do you think about the people in your life who have died? Who
do you think about most?

....

591 Who do you fear may be the next person to die in your circle of
friends or relatives?

....

592 Imagine you are told that you will die in a year's time. Would
you change anything about the way you live?

☐ yes   ☐ no

■ What would you change?

....

593 Imagine you are on your deathbed. Is there somebody you
would particularly want to talk to?

....

■ What would you say to that person?

....

■ Why have you not told them this already?

....

594 What is so important to you that without it your life would not be worth living?

....

595 Where would you like to be buried?

....

596 Three words that should be written on your gravestone:

597   Do you believe that suicide is wrong? Why?

....

....

598   What will change when you die?

....

....

599   What will die if you change?

....

....

FINAL QUESTIONS

600 Is this the best time of your life?

■ If yes, why?

....

■ If no, why not?

....

601 Have you found your place in life?

....

■ If yes, where or what is it?

....

602 Are you a good friend?

☐ yes ☐ no

603 Mark on the line: How deeply in love are you?

604   What are you good at?

....

....

605   Are you good at what you want to be good at?

....

....

606   Do you want to be good at what you're good at?

....

....

607   What do you want to be good at?

....

....

608   How high is your energy level?

609 As a percentage, how much time do you spend living in the past, in the present, in the future?

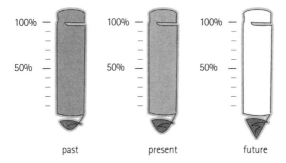

100% —	100% —	100% —
50% —	50% —	50% —
past	present	future

610 Think about your career so far. Mark on the career ladder:

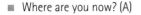

- Where are you now? (A)

- Where do you want to get to? (B)

- What is the highest rung you
  have reached? (C)

611 Describe yourself in three words.

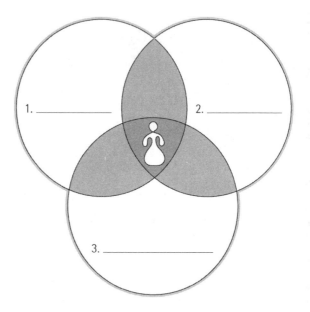

1. _____

2. _____

3. _____

12 Without worrying about your artistic abilities, draw something that represents you (animal, symbol, number, etc.).

613   What kind of journey are you on?

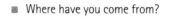

■ Where have you come from?

■ Where are you going to?

■ Who are you traveling with?

■ Who are you leaving behind?

■ What awaits you?

614 When did you last cry?

....

■ What about?

....

615 When was the last time you had a good laugh?

....

■ With whom?

....

616 What do you ask yourself again and again in life?

....

■ What is your current answer?

....

YOUR QUESTIONS

STILL GOT QUESTIONS?

The book has come to an end, but it isn't finished. What questions did you feel were missing? Can you think of other, better questions? Do you think we didn't go into enough depth with some subjects? Which questions made the strongest impression on you? Do you have a particularly interesting answer to one of the questions?

If you have any questions or comments, write to us: rt@guzo.ch or mk@kaospilot.dk.

On the Internet you'll find more great questions at: fragebuch.ch. You will also find videos of (famous) people answering questions for *The Question Book*.

You can find a version of this book for your iPhone/iPad in the iTunes App Store.

THANKS

This book could not have been written without the generous help of many people.

The book was read and tested by Simon Baumann, Dr. Eugen Häni, Marlène Iseli, Miriam Lenz, Jörg Scholz, and Solveig Scholz; the most intelligent questions were asked by Daniel Häni, Michael Krobath, Rebecca Lämmle, and Franziska Schutzbach; the initial ideas came from Andrea Schmidt; the best ideas came from Annamateur, Dag Grödal, Facebook, and Ondine Riesen; unsparing criticism was given by Senem Wicki; clichés were removed by Kenneth Domfe; stupid mistakes were prevented by Andreas "Becks" Dietrich; we were inspired by Mihaly Csikszentmihalyi, Lilli Binzegger, Rolf Dobelli, Max Frisch, Penelope Frohart, Philipp Keel, Thomas Meyer, Gary Poole, Marcel Proust, and Gregory Stock. The layout was designed by Anna Meyer, and the book was made possible, corrected, and improved by Laura Clemens and Peter Haag (Kein und Aber). The questions got their final touch by Lisa Owens, Profile.

Thanks in particular to Philip Earnhart for his clever illustrations.

▬ AUTHORS

Mikael Krogerus

Five films that are important to you:
The Rescuers, Audition, In the Mood for Love, Festen, Miller's Crossing

Five books that you love:
Okänd Soldat, Väinö Linna; *Blood Meridian*, Cormac McCarthy; *Money*, Martin Amis; *Embers*, Sándor Márai; *Stuff White People Like*, Christian Lander

Five types of people that annoy you:
Resentful, selfish, ambitious, insecure, humorless

Roman Tschäppeler

Five music albums that are important to you:
Back in Black, AC/DC; *Engelberg*, Stephan Eicher; *Just Like You*, Keb' Mo'; *Life on Planet Groove*, Maceo Parker; *Listen*, Urban Species

Five brands you like to buy:
Interio (only the Prologue notebooks), WE, PostFinance, Apple, Haribo

Five things you like to talk about at the moment:
Good ideas, infographics, stand-up comedy, my friends' music, recipes